Influence In Action™

Brings More Business to Entrepreneurs

By

Robert J. Smith, MFA,

Anish Verma, and

Leelan Rodriguez

Foreword by

Sharon L. Roznowski, M.Ed.

© Copyright 2024, Robert J. Smith, MFA. All rights reserved.

Book Layout ©2024. Published by: RJS Pro Publishing and Amazon Publishing Center.

No part of this book may be reproduced or transmitted in any form or by any means, electronic or mechanical, including photocopying, recording or by any information storage and retrieval system, without written permission from the authors, except for the inclusion of brief quotations in a review.

Limit of Liability Disclaimer: The information provided in this book is for informational purposes only and is not intended to be a source of direct consulting with respect to the material presented. The information and/or documents contained in this book do not constitute legal or financial advice and should never be used without first consulting a qualified advisor to determine which strategies may best fit your individual needs and be customized to your unique situation.

The publisher and the authors do not make any guarantee or other promise as to any results that may be obtained from using the content in this book. Meeting with a qualified advisor and conducting your own research and due diligence is always recommended. To the maximum extent permitted by law, the publisher and the authors disclaim any and all liability in the event any information, commentary, analysis, opinions, advice and/or recommendations contained in this book prove to be inaccurate, incomplete, unreliable, or result in any type of loss.

Content contained or made available through this book is not intended to constitute legal advice or financial advice, and no attorney-client relationship is formed through this published work.

Client relationships may only be formed at: https://SmithProfits.com/Services/

A no charge, no obligation consultation may be obtained at: **https://SmithProfits.com/Contact/**

Earnings Disclaimer: All income examples in this book are examples. They are not intended to represent or guarantee that everyone will achieve the same results. It is understood that each individual's success will be determined by his or her desire, dedication, background, effort, and motivation to work. There is no guarantee the reader will duplicate any of the results stated here. The reader recognizes that any and all business endeavors have inherent risk of loss of capital.

No Agency Relationship: The opinions of each co-author do not necessarily constitute the opinions of Robert J. Smith, Robert J. Smith Productions, or Smith Profits. Co-author content does not in any way constitute an agency relationship between any co-author and of Robert J. Smith, Robert J. Smith Productions, or Smith Profits.

Influence in Action™ Gains Proven Results and Drives Sales

1st Edition. 2024

ISBN (eBook): 978-1-965538-06-7

ISBN (Amazon Paperback): 978-1-965538-07-4

ISBN: (Amazon Hardcover): 978-1-965538-08-1

ISBN: (Ingram Spark Paperback): 978-1-965538-09-8

ISBN: (Ingram Spark Hardcover): 978-1-965538-20-3

ISBN: (Smashwords): 978-1-965538-10-4

TRADEMARKS: All product names, logos, and brands are the property of their respective owners. All company, product, and service names used in this book are for identification purposes only. Using these names, logos, and brands does not imply endorsement. All other trademarks cited herein are the property of their respective owners.

INFLUENCE IN ACTION™ has a Trademark pending International Class 016: Series of printed non-fiction books in the field of BUSINESS.

"**Reading furnishes the mind only with materials of knowledge; It is thinking that makes what we read, ours.**" -John Locke

We must do more than think; we must take intelligent *ACTION!*

When we take *ACTIONS* that have proven to *BRING MORE BUSINESS* to others, we *BRING MORE BUSINESS* to ourselves.

Dedication

To paraphrase the late great, George M. Cohan, as portrayed by my favorite actor, the late great, James Cagney;

My mother thanks you, my late great, father thanks you, my brother thanks you, my children thank you, my girlfriend thanks you, and I thank you.

Acknowledgments

As always, if it weren't for my family members who permit me the time to write, I wouldn't have any best-selling books or the opportunities that these books provide.

Thank you, Mom, Ron, Sharon, Ashley, Austin and Sabrina!

Thank you as well for your contributions to this book, Anish Verma and Leelan Rodriguez. Your individual work and moral ethics have surpassed many of your contemporaries who have come before you.

Each of your abilities to see projects through, combined with your commitment to keeping your word, will serve you well in both your careers and in your lives.

I would also like to take this opportunity to acknowledge each and every reader of this book and every book in my INFLUENCE IN ACTION™ series for your desire to succeed and your unwavering commitment to take ACTION to succeed with every proven principle in this book.

Thank you for leading the way, for referring others to this series and for providing them with the very same opportunity to succeed that you are taking for yourself.

Well done!

Contents

Dedication vii

Acknowledgments viii

Foreword xi

Prologue xv

Chapter One: Get Caught Up 1

Chapter Two: Friendly Persuasion....................................5

Chapter Three: Influence In Action™: 11

Chapter Four: Don't Trust the Process, Trust the Results .57

Chapter Five: Mindset of a Leader: 62

Chapter Six: The One Thing™ 87

Chapter Seven: Mentoring Matters 91

Chapter Eight: You Can Judge a Book by Its Cover 97

Epilogue 104

About Your Author 107

Foreword

By Sharon L. Roznowski, M.Ed.

In today's fast-paced world, the ability to influence has become a coveted and essential skill. It is not merely a tool for personal success but a vital force that shapes the very trajectory of our businesses, industries, and national economies. It is with great pleasure that I introduce you to Robert J. Smith, MFA, a true master of the art of influence.

With five decades of experience as a financial advisor, marketer, and sales powerhouse, Robert has navigated the ever-evolving landscape of business with a rare combination of both business and creativity. As a multi-million-dollar producer for some of the largest companies in America and around the globe, Robert has honed his craft, learning to harness the power of influence to drive remarkable results. He's also mastered the arts and the unlimited power of Factual Storytelling™ to achieve success with Fortune 500 Companies.

More important than his relentless pursuit of

achievement, where he has achieved #1 worldwide production rankings, is his passion to mentor and inspire countless others to reach new heights. In *INFLUENCE IN ACTION™ BRINGS MORE BUSINESS TO ENTREPRENEURS*, Robert shares the secrets of his success, laying bare the principles and strategies that have propelled him to the forefront of financial services and other industries.

At The Edison in Disney Springs

Whether you are an aspiring entrepreneur, a seasoned executive, or a professional seeking to elevate your impact, the lessons contained within these pages will be an invaluable guide that will help you cultivate your own brand of influence and propel you to heights you never thought possible. Prepare to embark on an exciting adventure where the power of influence becomes your greatest ally in the pursuit of business excellence.

With Robert as your trusted companion and advisor, you will discover the keys to unlocking your full potential. You will gain the ability to quickly shape your future with the force of your ideas, your vision, and your ability to inspire others. Together, using many of his proven strategies, Robert and I were able to generate a positive influence within my classroom and beyond. I'm excited for you to experience the same results! Get ready to be influenced. Get ready to influence!

Elementary School Book Character Parade

Prologue

We All Have the Ability to Take ACTION Without Limitation

Our ability to take ACTION is not limited by age.

Pablo Picasso was a prolific painter who continued to work and produce fine art until the day he died at the age of 91 on April 8, 1973.

Only last night (as of this writing), we saw Mike Tyson, a 58-year-old man, go the distance in an eight-round-bout against 27-year-old Jake Paul in the prime of his life. "Iron Mike" accomplished this feat through months of consistent ACTION, training each and every day, doing things that most people would never even consider attempting. This is only five to six months out from being hospitalized for a bleeding ulcer.

While this was an exhibition bout, the fact remains that at age 58, Tyson defended 278 punches from Paul, and 78 of those punches landed. While millions of people are already criticizing both heavyweights, how many of us have ever defended 278 punches and been hit 78 times in our entire lives, much less in one night with more than 60 million people watching? "You saw him. He tripped when he was walking down to the ring. He had a hard time walking up the stairs. He had a knee brace on, and Jake Paul still couldn't do anything to him." -Dana White, CEO and President of the UFC.

And the debate rages on. Did Paul actually beat "Iron Mike," or did Tyson hold back for a $20 million payoff so that he could take care of his family? This is where the smart money is. We all saw Tyson repeatedly pull his punches and simply stand in front of Paul, taking everything that the youngster had for him. Any way you look at it, at the age of 58, Mike Tyson was able to achieve a $20 million payday, working in a "young man's game."

On the other end of the age spectrum, a young high school student I worked with, Davina Horowitz, won two entrepreneur pitch competitions at the tender age of 14. She earned her second victory less than seven months ago. To do so, Davina also took consistent ACTION, working on and improving a pitch for the medical device that she created. Like Mike, Davina has the discipline to do what the majority of her peers are either unable or unwilling to do. That is, take consistent ACTION to accomplish her goal. She's perfecting her medical device while attending school.

Our ability to take ACTION is also not limited by our health or circumstances.

Take my friend, Leelan Rodriguez, for example. You'll see his story here in Chapter Four. He didn't let a life-changing accident deter him from taking consistent ACTION, and he never will.

Same with my friend, Steven Berkani, who was born with cerebral palsy, which has confined him to a wheelchair for life. None of these challenges has stopped Steven from doing incredible work as an independent film maker who creates Public Service Announcements (PSAs) for the benefit of all mankind. Steven's story may be found here: https://wgntv.com/business/press-releases/ein-presswire/652921909/filmmaker-defies-cerebral-palsy-and-conquers-challenges-to-ignite-change/

Even if you are not fortunate enough to know these fine people, simply look at our American history for a story of great perseverance in the most difficult of circumstances.

Helen Keller, with the help of Annie Sullivan, was able to overcome extreme difficulties, such as losing her sight, hearing, and ability to communicate. This happened at the age of only 19 months when she contracted a life-threatening illness. If you know anything at all about her story, you know that she overcame her extreme difficulties through daily, consistent ACTION. In fact, she became a well-known humanitarian, educator and writer. Helen Keller worked diligently to aid others affected by blindness and advocated for women's suffrage. Helen Keller also co-founded the American Civil Liberties Union (ACLU).

I'm totally and permanently disabled, myself. Neither that fact nor anything else will ever stop me from taking consistent ACTION as long as I have breath in my body. I hope that the same goes for everyone who reads this book. In short, nothing can stop any of us from taking consistent action; once we make up our minds, nothing can stop us.

If you or anyone you know has a story that will inspire others, by all means, share it. You never know who may benefit from it. If you'd like to recommend anyone, including yourself, for a chapter in one of our subsequent books, feel free to reach out to me at Smith Profits.

https://SmithProfits.com

"The intelligence consists not only in the knowledge, but also, in the skill to apply the knowledge into practice." - Aristotle

Influence In Action™

Chapter One:
Get Caught Up

Like a 1970s TV show, let's review what happened in ***INFLUENCE IN ACTION*™ *GAINS PROVEN RESULTS AND DRIVES SALES.***

In the opening book of this #1 Best Selling series, we learned to:

Always keep our word. When your clients and everyone around you know that you are a man or woman of your word, there is truly no limit to what you are able to accomplish.

Always take ACTION. All of the knowledge in the world is of little use to any of us unless we take consistent ACTION to put that knowledge to use. We are obliged to put our knowledge to effective use for everyone around us as well as for ourselves.

Develop effective Factual Storytelling™ methods. Through these proven methods, I truly believe that anyone and everyone is capable of achieving great heights in business and in life.

Become a superhero to our clients. I've had the very good fortune to have clients tell me that I saved their businesses, homes, and marriages simply by helping them improve how they do what they do for a living. It's very rewarding to know that you've helped people. If you've already done good for people, you already know. If you haven't had the opportunity to be of massive benefit to others yet, you soon will.

Optimize our LinkedIn profile. When you improve your Social Selling Index on LinkedIn, sales improve. You gain more sales and larger sales with ease. It really is that simple.

Utilize the Internet Movie Database (IMDb) to be at the top of the front page of Google searches. If you haven't yet created a strategy to leverage podcasts and other appearances to gain top of Google search rankings in order to become more visible and gain more customers and clients, we can help.

Make the most of authority marketing. You've learned how to gain instant credibility with your prospects, customers, and clients. You've also learned how to grow and maintain your credibility.

Make the most of scarcity marketing. You learned how to create valid scarcity to ethically earn more business.

Maintain consistency. We all know that consistency is key to optimal performance. We also know that consistency helps to create, build and maintain momentum.

Smile our way to profits. We learned the importance of smiling, liking others and helping others to like us as well. Business, advertising, and public relations are largely built on these simple concepts.

Make the most of affiliation marketing and benefit from customer conformity. We learned affiliate marketing to benefit from our human nature and stand with those we feel united with. I've had the pleasure of enjoying five decades of referrals as a result of natural consensus.

Expect referrals to generate referrals. The setting of high expectations is key. Most businesspeople do the opposite. They set out to "manage expectations" merely by setting low expectations. If there was ever a recipe for failure, this is it. The best business comes from setting high expectations and meeting or exceeding those expectations.

Play the percentages. In order to play the percentages, we must first know the percentages. I must know, understand, and master the fundamentals of our business. We must also be lifelong students of human nature. We must know what to expect from every business and life dealing. We must know how to think on our feet.

Here's a bonus strategy: Find someone who has accomplished the things you want to accomplish. Seek out that person's advice, whether through mentoring, consulting, coaching or whatever route suits you best. Apply strategies that have been proven to work. Work with strategies that your selected advisor has proven to work through his or her own application and success. This is what the high school and medical school students we have worked with have done. So far, these students who follow our methods are UNDEFEATED in their Entrepreneur pitch competitions.

Here's another bonus strategy: Be prolific. Forget the stale Glengarry Glen Ross line, 'ABC, Always Be Closing.' Instead, remember ABP, *Always Be Producing*. Producing products, services, articles, books, etc. Whatever it is that you do, do a lot of it, and do it well. Be prolific.

Chapter Two:
Friendly Persuasion

In my Forbes magazine article, *'Friendly Persuasion': The Psychology Of Influence*, I wrote:

The best tagline for the film *Friendly Persuasion*, which featured Gary Cooper, Dorothy McGuire and Anthony Perkins as the Birdwells, a family of pacifists drawn into the American Civil War, was "Try *FRIENDLY PERSUASION:* It's powerful!" I was so impressed with this movie promotion that I tried it.

As you may have noticed from **INFLUENCE IN ACTION™ GAINS PROVEN RESULTS AND DRIVES SALES**, my Forbes series consists of movie and television themes to illustrate proven principles to help readers achieve massive business success through their consistent application in our day-to-day work.

It is commonly held that influence and persuasion consist of reciprocity, scarcity, authority, consistency, liking, social proof and unity. Here's how I've made these

Robert J. Smith, MFA

proven principles work for maximum client acquisition and sales over the past three decades:

Authority - As Will Rogers purportedly said, "You never get a second chance to make a first impression." Most often, a prospective client's first impression of you and your business will come from your website. Be sure to include all major network television logos and other media brands on your website to denote coverage and add necessary credibility.

Make sure, as I have always done, that your biography includes all of your academic credentials and professional designations, such as BBA, MBA, MFA, PhD, RIA, CLU, CHFC, LIC, AAMS, etc.

If your website is set up correctly and it's done its job, your prospect will book an initial consultation through your site. You're on your way to the next step.

Reciprocity - Prior to your discovery interview or first appointment, provide your prospect with a gift of value. Only a gift of proven value will work to invoke this principle. For example, provide your prospects a gift of *INFLUENCE IN ACTION™*.

Influence In Action™

To stay in the top 1% of worldwide financial services ranking, we used to mail out hard copies of *THE ADVENTURES OF INSURANCEMAN©* marketing and sales comic that I wrote about a superhero insurance agent who explained complex topics in an easy-to-understand manner. Hard copies have been known to have a shelf life of years, and I've found they also tend to get passed on to other potential clients. We've never found or created a better tool for obtaining referrals.

These are upfront gifts of value that use sales psychology to increase client acquisition and sales through storytelling and research-based evidence. These gifts invoke a social obligation to return the favor by making prospects and clients more likely to buy and invest as well as to refer new businesses.

Always attach a welcome letter to your gift in order to set expectations for your initial and subsequent appointments. Your welcome letter should include content with two or three of these essential elements of persuasion.

Scarcity- Key points to get across: I can only meet with so many people in a year. Each prospective client gets only one shot to do business with me. I'm far too busy for second chances. I am in demand, and my time is limited. It's a simple truth. This truth is confirmed by my calendar, which is posted on our primary website, and you can do the same by sharing your availability on your own website. Avoid any trendy and overused false scarcity tactics such as "limited time" and "this offer ends ... never to return." Sophisticated buyers see through such tired and blatantly false tactics.

Consistency - Include examples of generational clients. Gain coverage on multiple television networks, newspapers, magazines and even podcast streaming services. Display this coverage on your websites, in email signatures, and on other marketing pieces to improve closing ratios during discovery and subsequent interviews.

Liking - Clients repeatedly refer to businesses and advisors they like and trust. This also sets the stage for referrals to be earned and expected. Tell clients stories of other clients who have referred you and how well you made those clients look at work, their country club, in their neighborhood, etc.

Social Proof - Gain celebrity and/or industry endorsements as evidence that you are a trusted source and a go-to person in your industry. For example, on our landing page, we include an endorsement from an original Shark from Shark

Tank. There is no better authority than a referral from a satisfied client. Qualified referrals should be closed 100% of the time.

In addition to using media sources that provide instant social proof, client success stories should also be used. For example: "We saved a Massachusetts picture framing company over $65,000 in annual business taxes after discovering a deduction that their CPA missed for 20 years running."

Unity - Work with affinity groups of clients such as medical societies, school districts, professional athletes, etc.

All of this preparation upfront fully prepares prospects to freely accept your message before you deliver it to them. Their defenses are down, and you have placed yourself in an optimal position to gain them as a new client. It then becomes your primary focus to service them to the best of your ability so that you earn maximum referrals from them. Every time you hit a home run for them, ask them who they know who can benefit from similar successes.

We may not be of the *Friendly Persuasion*, and we hope to never have to battle through another American Civil

War like the Birdwell family did. However, we can all rest assured that the art of friendly and ethical persuasion can help you reach new heights in your business and in your industry, as it did for me.

Chapter Three:
Influence In Action™:
The Neuroscience Of Inspirational Leadership

Author: Anish A. Verma

Leadership is more than a title; it's about the ability to influence and inspire action. In business, leaders who can inspire others to achieve results far beyond what's possible through simple motivation will be more successful and have a more fulfilling career. The difference between inspiring and motivating lies in the depth of connection, the longevity of impact, and the unity that a shared vision brings.

Inspiration is not just a burst of energy; it's a transformative force that plants a seed of purpose within each team member, which grows into a lasting commitment to a shared vision. In contrast, motivation is that burst of energy — it can propel people forward but fades if not reinforced by habits and deeper connections.

Robert J. Smith, MFA

John Maxwell, a renowned leader and team-building expert and the author of more than 75 books, defines leadership in simple terms: "Leadership is influence, nothing more, nothing less." This definition underscores the immense power that leaders hold. Influence is at the heart of inspirational leadership. Leaders who inspire don't rely on their title or authority to guide people; they rely on their ability to influence, connect, and move others toward a shared vision. This encapsulates the essence of what it means to lead with inspiration.

Inspiring leaders can influence those around them by building trust, fostering strong relationships, and demonstrating unwavering integrity. These qualities are not just desirable but crucial for effective leadership. They understand that leadership is not a one-way street; it's a constant exchange of energy, ideas, and values. By influencing others positively, these leaders create a ripple effect that extends far beyond their immediate circle, reassuring others of their steadfast commitment.

Consider the story of Howard Schultz, former CEO of Starbucks. When he returned to Starbucks in 2008 during a crisis, he didn't just give motivational speeches; he reignited a sense of purpose within the company. Schultz inspired his employees to focus on quality coffee and customer experience, emphasizing a return to Starbucks' roots. This internal connection helped the team weather the recession and regain focus, leading to sustainable growth.

As leaders, it is crucial to understand how to tap into this deeper well of inspiration. The first and most important step in doing so is becoming self-aware. Only by understanding how our conscious and subconscious minds operate can we begin to influence others effectively. This chapter delves into how self-awareness enables leaders to INSPIRE, how motivation differs from inspiration, how the brain functions, a forgotten brain link to reinforce why motivation fades, and how information alone is not enough to create a lasting change. For example, everyone knows how to lose weight – eat less, exercise more, and sleep well. But how many people actually lose weight? We all get motivated to set up resolutions, but what happens next? "My leadership coach always says – it is not what you know, it is what you do with what you know. Everyone wants to be a great leader, but how many actually work on becoming one?

Robert J. Smith, MFA

The Power of Inspiration vs. the Mechanics of Motivation

Motivation and inspiration are words often used interchangeably, but their effects on individuals and teams are worlds apart. Motivation tends to be transactional and short-term, frequently driven by external factors like rewards, deadlines, or consequences. Picture a boss who motivates a team by setting strict targets, offering bonuses for hitting numbers, or threatening consequences for underperformance. The team may indeed perform, but the performance is tied to the external reward or fear of failure.

Inspiration, on the other hand, is transformational. It doesn't push people to act; it pulls them toward something more significant. Leaders who inspire create a vision that resonates with people's internal drives and sense of purpose. They foster an environment where individuals want to perform not because they have to but because they feel compelled to contribute to something meaningful. As John Quincy Adams, the 6th US president, once said, "If your actions inspire others to dream more, learn more, do more, and become more, you are a leader."

Let's evaluate how the Oxford Dictionary defines these words and their origins.

- Motivate, verb
  - Definition: To induce (a person) to act in a certain way; to provide (a person, organization, etc.) with a motive or incentive to do something.
  - Origin: The word motivate comes from the Latin word "movere," which means "to move."
- Inspire, verb
  - Definition: To 'breathe in' or infuse (a feeling, thought, principle, etc.) into the mind or soul.
  - Origin: This word may be traced back to the Latin "inspirare" ("to breathe or blow into"), which itself is from the word "spirare," meaning "to breathe."

As mentioned earlier, the difference between inspiring and motivating lies in the depth of connection and the longevity of impact. Motivation is an external force that helps or moves you to do something. It works and serves its purpose, but its effect is temporary. Think of your New Year's resolution to lose weight as an example. Or a training program where you learn new techniques. Your neocortex, the sensory part of your brain responsible for conscious thought, gets stimulated. The thought then finds an emotional connection in the limbic brain, which is your emotion and motivation hub, and you, in that environment, feel highly motivated and on fire. You love the new ideas and are excited to apply the latest strategies you learned, but you will often automatically default to your old behavior after a few days. This happens based on how your brain functions and how you are wired. The neocortex part of the brain aligns with your conscious mind, which can think of unlimited thoughts, but its capacity is limited to process and analyze them. When you understand why your brain functions the way it does, how and what you do will become more evident.

On the other hand, inspiration involves breathing something into you, like lighting your inner flame and connecting at a deeper level. It either aligns with your feelings and belief systems or helps you overcome your limiting beliefs. Because it is more internal and connected to your limbic brain, the emotional part of your brain that deals with your feelings, emotions, habits, fears, and beliefs, any changes made and repeated again and again will tend to become more permanent. The limbic brain is part of the subconscious mind. The subconscious mind has unlimited capacity and is always working. 90% of our decisions and actions are automatic and conducted via the subconscious mind. The subconscious mind does not reason and cannot understand language. It just goes to work to convert whatever is put in there via repetition, manifesting itself in the real world. Ergo, when something is lit inside you at a deep emotional level, you will tend to repeat it enough times to make it a habit. And since habits reside in your subconscious mind, you will tend to repeat those actions automatically without effort.

In summary, motivation will cause you to act. You will prioritize your new learnings via your conscious mind, but life will come in the way, and you will default to your old behavior. That is how the conscious mind works. It always pays attention to the most urgent and essential things, and because it has limited capacity, it will continue to shuffle your priorities, causing your motivation to fade. Unless that motivation strikes a chord deep inside you and inspires you, you won't focus on taking intentional action and won't repeat it enough to make it a habit and transfer it into your subconscious mind. Remember, the subconscious mind has unlimited capacity and does things with the least effort.

Whether you are trying to lose weight, build better relationships at home, or want to be an effective leader at work or your business, the above principles apply.

Robert J. Smith, MFA

The Hourglass of Career Evolution: Broadening Skills for Inspirational Leadership

One of my managers, way early in my career, gave me an analogy of how our career paths evolve and how leadership skills must adjust correspondingly. He used an example of an hourglass.

As we navigate our professional journeys, our careers often resemble the shape of an hourglass, symbolizing the dynamic shift between the breadth and depth of skills over time. Understanding this evolution is crucial for leaders who aim to inspire and connect with their teams effectively.

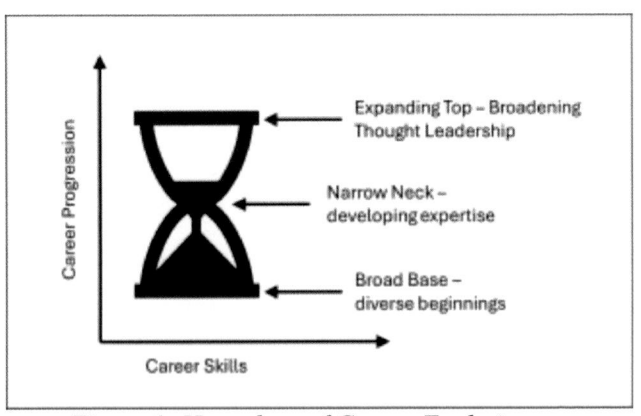

Figure 1: Hourglass of Career Evolution

Influence In Action™

The Broad Base: Diverse Beginnings

At the outset of our careers, we typically start with a broad focus. We're like sponges, eager to absorb knowledge across various domains. This phase is characterized by:

- Exploration and Learning: We engage in different roles, projects, and tasks, gaining exposure to multiple aspects of the business or industry.

- Skill Acquisition: A wide range of skills are developed, from technical abilities to understanding organizational processes.

- Finding Our Path: Through diverse experiences, we begin to identify our interests and strengths.

For example, a young marketing professional might dabble in content creation, social media management, market research, and event planning. This exploratory stage is essential for building a foundation of knowledge and understanding how different puzzle pieces fit together.

The Narrow Neck: Developing Expertise

As we progress, there's a natural narrowing of focus. We start to specialize and become experts in specific areas.

This stage involves:

- Deepening Knowledge: We delve deeper into a particular field, honing our expertise.
- Building Credibility: Specialized skills lead to recognition as a subject matter expert.
- Increased Responsibility: With expertise comes more significant projects and complex challenges.

Continuing the earlier example, our marketing professional might focus solely on digital marketing analytics, becoming an expert in interpreting data to drive marketing strategies. This specialization is akin to moving through the neck of the hourglass, where our skills are concentrated and highly focused.

The Expanding Top: Broadening Thought Leadership

Upon reaching a certain level of expertise, many professionals transition into leadership roles. Here, the career path widens again:

- Shift from Technical to Soft Skills: Technical expertise becomes less central as leadership abilities take precedence.

- Managing Teams: Leaders oversee diverse groups, requiring skills in communication, empathy, and influence.
- Strategic Visioning: The focus expands to include organizational goals, culture building, and long-term planning.

At this point, our marketing expert may become a Marketing Director, responsible not just for analytics but for guiding a whole team, setting department goals, and aligning with the company's vision. This upper widening of the hourglass signifies the importance of soft skills in leadership.

If you are reading this book, you are either at the narrow neck of the hourglass or have begun your progression towards the expanding top of broader thought leadership. You are a high-performing executive leading one functional team and a sought-after, well-established subject matter expert. Irrespective of where you are, you will find this book helpful to moving you onward and upward.

Leaders who succeed in the broader thought leadership section of the hourglass need to begin the transition into a heightened level of self-awareness. Based on a study conducted by Ohio State University on Leader Self-Awareness, self-aware leaders tend to perform better, have higher levels of leadership effectiveness, and are more likely to be promoted. This is because self-aware leaders have more accurate knowledge about their strengths and weaknesses, have positive attitudes toward feedback, and set goals to improve their performance.

These inspirational leaders recognize that the skills that led to success as an individual contributor and as a subject matter expert may not be the ones needed to be a high-performing leader to manage teams and organizations. They need to be aware of their automatic behaviors and adjust them to better serve the team and organization. They need to reflect on one's leadership style and its effectiveness continuously. They must have a keen sense of their strengths by leveraging Acumax, DISC, or Strength Finder assessments.

For instance, the skilled marketing professional manager might realize that their tendency to micromanage—effectively ensuring personal work quality—can hinder team growth. By applying self-awareness, they can shift towards empowering the team members and fostering innovation and engagement.

The hourglass doesn't signify a one-time transformation but an ongoing process. These inspirational leaders embrace continuous growth. They are lifelong learners who must continue to learn and adapt, embracing new ideas and approaches. They always work on expanding their influence on the more significant parts of the organization, requiring even broader skills. They nurture and empower others to cultivate future leaders, help shape the next generation and continue the cycle.

The Three Brains and Leadership

Before understanding how high performers become influential and inspirational leaders, we must know how our brains function at the executive level and how different brain regions interact. The human brain is highly complex and the most critical organ. It has 100 billion neurons and trillions of supporting cells. The brain has more connections than stars in the universe. It is 2% of the body weight, consumes 20% - 30% of calories and 20% of oxygen and blood flow.

For this chapter, we will break down the brain into three

major components: Neocortex, the Limbic brain, and the Motor brain, and explain 'The Forgotten Link.'

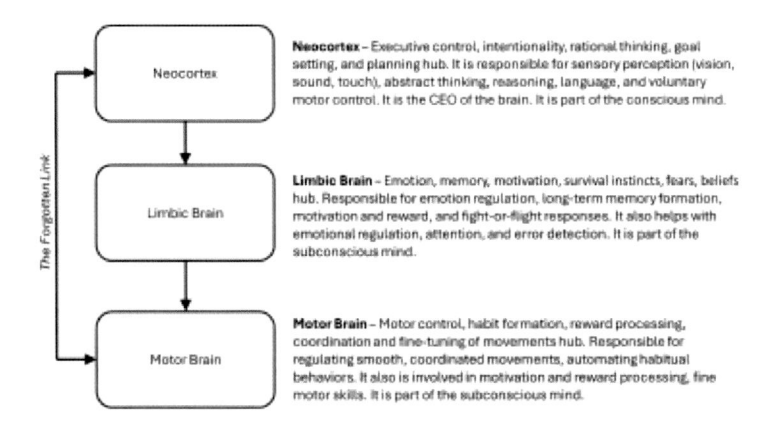

Neocortex – Executive control, intentionality, rational thinking, goal setting, and planning hub. It is responsible for sensory perception (vision, sound, touch), abstract thinking, reasoning, language, and voluntary motor control. It is the CEO of the brain. It is part of the conscious mind.

Limbic Brain – Emotion, memory, motivation, survival instincts, fears, beliefs hub. Responsible for emotion regulation, long-term memory formation, motivation and reward, and fight-or-flight responses. It also helps with emotional regulation, attention, and error detection. It is part of the subconscious mind.

Motor Brain – Motor control, habit formation, reward processing, coordination and fine-tuning of movements hub. Responsible for regulating smooth, coordinated movements, automating habitual behaviors. It also is involved in motivation and reward processing, fine motor skills. It is part of the subconscious mind.

Figure 2: Key brain regions

Figure 2 illustrates these three major regions of the brain and their key roles and functions. They are also organized based on how these structures appear in the brain and how they interact with each other.

Understanding the intricate workings of the brain can be simplified by comparing its regions to the various departments and roles within a business organization. This analogy helps illustrate how different parts of the brain collaborate to achieve seamless operation, much like a well-coordinated company. Below, we'll explore the three key brain regions and their sub-components and will explain their functions using business terminology:

1. Neocortex as the Executive Leadership and Innovation Hub

2. Limbic Brain is the Emotion and Motivation hub

3. Motor Brain as the Operations and Production Hub.

1. Neocortex – The Executive Leadership and Innovation Hub

Neocortex – The Strategic Leader's Tool:

- The neocortex is the brain's thinking cap—it's where leaders analyze data, strategize, and make deliberate choices. This is the part of the conscious mind where rational thought and planning occur.

- Example: Jeff Bezos at Amazon uses the neocortex's strength when making data-driven decisions. Amazon's obsession with customer data and long-term thinking is a direct reflection of neocortex-driven leadership. Bezos used strategic focus to build a customer-centric culture.

- How It Connects to Leadership: Leaders use their neocortex to create strategic visions, but to inspire, they must move beyond rational thought and engage the emotional center of their team members.

    Business Analogy:

- The Executive Leadership and Innovation Department combines the roles of CEO and Strategic Planning Team.

- Functions:

    o Strategic Vision: Sets the organization's overall direction and long-term goals.

    o Decision-Making: Analyzes information to make informed decisions.

    o Innovation: Generates new ideas and strategies for growth and improvement.

    o Problem-Solving: Addresses complex challenges and develops solutions.

Influence In Action™

Explanation:

- The Neocortex (Executive Leadership) processes information from various sources to guide the organization's strategic decisions.
- It integrates data, assesses risks, and formulates plans that align with the company's mission and objectives.
- Example: Deciding to enter a new market after analyzing market trends and competitive landscapes.

2. **Limbic Brain – The Emotion and Motivation Hub**

   Limbic Brain – The Emotional Connection:

   - The limbic brain is the heart of emotions. It doesn't understand words but responds to stories, feelings, and shared experiences, making it key to inspirational leadership.
   - Example: Simon Sinek's famous concept of "Start with Why" emphasizes that great leaders inspire by connecting with the limbic brain of their audience. Apple's ability to inspire a sense of creativity and

innovation comes not from their products alone but from their emotional message of thinking differently.

- How It Connects to Leadership: To truly inspire, leaders need to speak to the limbic brain by sharing their vision in a way that resonates emotionally. This is what creates lasting change.

Business Analogy:

- The Human Resources (HR) and Company Culture Department
- Functions:
  - Employee Engagement: Fosters a positive work environment and culture.
  - Motivation: Implements programs to motivate and reward employees.
  - Emotional Well-being: Supports employees' emotional and mental health.
  - Relationship Building: Promotes teamwork and collaboration.

Influence In Action™

Explanation:

- The Limbic Brain (HR Department) manages the emotional climate of the organization.
- It ensures that employees are motivated, engaged, and aligned with the company's values.
- Example: Organizing team-building activities to strengthen relationships and boost morale.

3. **Motor Brain – The Operations and Production Unit**

   Motor Brain – Turning Inspiration into Action:

   - The motor brain helps turn inspired ideas into daily habits. This part of the subconscious mind is responsible for automating actions through repetition.
   - Example: At Toyota, the practice of continuous improvement (Kaizen) becomes automatic for employees through daily rituals and routines. Leaders at Toyota don't just tell workers to "improve"; they embed improvement practices into the daily workflow, turning inspired ideas into automated habits.

- How It Connects to Leadership: The motor brain ensures that the inspiration provided by the leader translates into consistent action. It allows a vision to be realized through routine.

Business Analogy:

- The Operations and Production Unit
- Functions:
  - Process Automation: Streamlines and automates routine tasks for efficiency.
  - Quality Control: Ensures products and services meet quality standards.
  - Coordination: Synchronizes various operational activities.
  - Continuous Improvement: Refines processes based on feedback and performance data.

Explanation:

- The Motor Brain (Operations and Production Unit) is responsible for executing tasks efficiently and effectively.

- Automates routine tasks, allowing the organization to operate smoothly without constant oversight.
- Fine-tune and coordinate actions to ensure high-quality outputs.
- Example: Implementing standardized procedures for manufacturing to ensure consistent product quality.

What is 'The Forgotten Link'? Let's use examples to elaborate on the role of the three brain regions and the forgotten link. Learning to ride a bicycle is a classic example of how the neocortex, limbic brain, and motor brain work together seamlessly. Initially, the neocortex engages as you consciously process instructions and strategize how to balance and pedal. You focus intently on keeping your eyes forward, maintaining a steady pedaling rhythm, and avoiding obstacles—all requiring deliberate thought and planning. Simultaneously, the limbic brain influences your emotions, perhaps mixing excitement with a bit of fear. Motivation might come from the encouragement of a parent or the anticipation of joining friends on bike rides. As you practice, the motor brain begins to take over, coordinating your movements and gradually automating the actions required to balance, steer, and pedal. Through repetition, these movements become smoother and require less conscious effort. Eventually, riding a bicycle becomes second nature; the motor brain handles the complex coordination automatically, allowing the neocortex to focus on other things, like enjoying the scenery, while the limbic brain experiences the joy and freedom of cycling.

It's the motor brain that ultimately transforms conscious effort into automatic skill, turning the deliberate actions of balancing and pedaling into the effortless joy of cycling. However, without you being intentional and without multiple repetitions, the link between your intention and your motor brain is not established. Unless this link strengthens, your motor brain will not learn how to drive a bicycle, and so will you.

By automating the complex coordination required to ride a bicycle, the motor brain allows you to shift from painstakingly thinking about every movement to enjoying the ride instinctively. This highlights the importance of the forgotten link and the motor brain's vital role in solidifying learned behaviors into seamless, subconscious abilities.

Influence In Action™

Now, let's apply this to a corporate setting. At Acme Tech Inc., a software company facing stagnant sales, the leadership team decided to implement a new consultative selling strategy to better meet client needs. The neocortex, representing executive leadership, developed this strategy by analyzing market trends and customer feedback and creating a detailed plan with clear objectives for the sales team. To ensure success, they needed the limbic brain's influence, akin to the company's human resources and culture department, to motivate and secure the team's emotional buy-in. Leadership communicated the benefits of the new approach, shared success stories, and addressed any fears or concerns, fostering enthusiasm and commitment. After initial pushback and resistance from the sales team, they began practicing the new consultative techniques, and the motor brain came into play. Through repeated use of pre-call planning, client discussions, and post-call reviews, these new behaviors started to become habitual. The forgotten link gets strengthened and creates deeper pathways in your motor brain. Over time, the consultative selling approach became ingrained in the team's routines, requiring less conscious effort and allowing them to focus more on client relationships. This integration of strategic planning, emotional engagement, and habit formation led to improved sales performance, enhanced team morale, and stronger client relationships, demonstrating how the collaboration of the neocortex, limbic brain, and motor brain drives successful organizational change.

The motor brain's role was pivotal in embedding the new consultative selling approach into daily habits, transforming a strategic initiative into a sustained, automatic practice that drove lasting sales success. However, without intention or inspiration, the link between the neocortex and the motor brain remains weak. In the case of the bicycle example, the purpose is clear: you are learning to ride a bicycle, which means independence and fun.

In this corporate example, the inspiration to be intentional will come only when the sales team understands what is in it for them. The inspiration will light up their inner flame and create a pull instead of being motivated by reward or fear.

Through intention, repetition, and practice, the motor brain enabled the sales team to internalize the new behaviors, making the consultative approach a natural part of client interactions. This underscores the importance of the motor brain in converting deliberate changes into habitual actions, making them second nature and moving them to a subconscious level that fuels organizational growth.

How does enough repetition engage the motor brain in forming habits? Why is understanding this pathway important? Let's do a quick review.

1. Initially, the Limbic brain provides emotional motivation (e.g., excitement from a conference).

2. The Neocortex helps translate that motivation into a plan and maintains focus on repeating the new behavior.

3. The reward system (through dopamine release) provides positive reinforcement, encouraging you to continue the behavior.

4. With intention, inspiration, and repetition, the forgotten link gets stronger and creates new pathways in your brain.

5. As you keep repeating the behavior over days and weeks, the motor brain begins to encode, pathways

in the brain get deeper, and then the action becomes an automatic habit, taking over control of the behavior and reducing the cognitive effort needed.

Motivation alone isn't enough to form habits. It can start the process, but consistent effort driven by the Neocortex and reinforced by the brain's reward system is necessary for long-term change. The Neocortex acts as a coach, keeping the new behavior on track until the motor brain can automate it. You need accountability partners (calendar systems, habit-tracking apps, or actual people) or coaches to keep you on track and strengthen the forgotten link to ensure you consistently repeat the steps before the motor brain takes over. Dopamine, a neurotransmitter, plays a key role in this process. It is released when you experience pleasure or reward, like completing a task or seeing progress. By making the process enjoyable or satisfying, dopamine rewards help bridge the gap between effortful repetition and automatic habits, strengthening the forgotten link.

To make the most of external motivation and build habits:

a. Use the Limbic brain to leverage the emotional spark by immediately setting a specific goal (e.g., "I will walk 10 minutes daily").

b. Engage the Neocortex to create a routine and reminders to keep yourself accountable, using tools like calendars or habit-tracking apps.

c. Leverage rewards and give yourself small rewards for sticking to the routine (e.g., enjoying a favorite podcast while exercising).

d. Repeat the action consistently, strengthening the link between intention and motor brain until it becomes automatic, allowing the motor brain to take over.

By understanding this pathway, you can better manage how initial motivation is translated into lasting habits, making behavioral change more sustainable and less dependent on temporary bursts of motivation.

So now you understand not just how your brain works but why it works the way it does. You now know that the forgotten link and the motor brain explain why your motivation fades and why you default to your old behaviors.

Robert J. Smith, MFA

When the 'why' becomes clear, the 'how' and 'what' become much easier to execute. Figure 3 summarizes this entire section and how you can utilize it to apply it to your personal and professional situation.

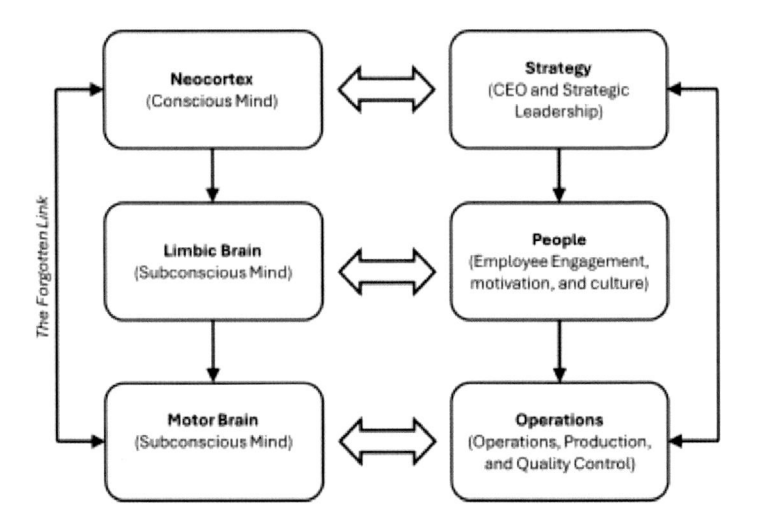

Figure 3: Key brain regions explained in business terms

- **Neocortex (Strategic leadership):** This region sets the direction and analyzes trends, helping the CEO and the company make smart decisions and long-term plans.

- **Limbic Brain (People, HR and Motivation):** This region drives emotional engagement and motivation, ensuring the team is motivated and aligned with the company's culture.

- **The Forgotten Link (Inspiration & Intention):** Helps you repeat actions, despite your limbic brain fears and limiting beliefs, to create new pathways in your brain until the motor brain can deepen the pathway and automate it

- **Motor Brain (Operations and Production):** Turns plans into action, automates routine processes, and maintains quality in execution.

Together, these regions form a high-functioning organization that can adapt to new challenges, stay motivated, and execute strategies effectively. The success of this "company" relies on how well these departments collaborate, with each other providing unique value to ensure that big ideas translate into real-world success. When you apply this to yourself, you know how to take your ideas and motivation, use action, and translate them into v2.0 of yourself.

Robert J. Smith, MFA

Unveiling INSPIRE: The Neuroscience of Transformational Leadership:

In the journey to becoming an inspirational leader, understanding the interplay between leadership principles and brain function is paramount. To simplify this complex relationship, we've distilled the essential elements of inspirational leadership into a powerful acronym: **INSPIRE**. Each letter represents a core attribute that not only defines effective leadership but also aligns with specific neurological processes within the **neocortex**, **limbic brain**, and **motor brain**.

The **INSPIRE** model encapsulates:

- I – Intentionality
- N – Nurture
- S – Self-Awareness
- P – Purpose
- I – Influence
- R – Resilience
- E – Empower

By exploring each component, we'll delve into how these leadership qualities engage different regions of the brain, bridging the gap between the conscious and subconscious minds. This synergy enhances your ability to lead with clarity, connect emotionally with your team, and foster habits that drive sustained success.

In the following sections, we'll unpack each element of the INSPIRE acronym. We'll examine how Intentionality leverages strategic thinking in the neocortex, how Nurture fosters emotional bonds through the limbic brain, and how Empower activates the motor brain to develop new skills and habits within your team.

Embracing the INSPIRE model enables you to transform not only your leadership approach but also the performance and engagement of those you lead. It's an invitation to harness the full potential of your brain—and theirs—to create a lasting, positive impact within your organization.

Let's embark on this exploration of the **INSPIRE** principles and discover how neuroscience validates the power of inspirational leadership.

Robert J. Smith, MFA

INSPIRE Acronym Explained

I – Intentionality

Intentionality involves acting with purpose, deliberate focus, and clarity of vision. It means setting clear goals and aligning actions to achieve those goals consistently. For leaders, it's about being proactive rather than reactive, making conscious choices that drive the organization forward. Intentionality encompasses vision creation, goal setting, and the ability to communicate that vision effectively to inspire others.

- Vision Creation and Communication: Developing and articulating a compelling vision that provides direction and purpose for the organization.

- Goal Setting: Defining specific, measurable, achievable, relevant, and time-bound (SMART) goals that serve as milestones toward realizing the vision.

- Strategic Planning: Crafting strategies that align resources and efforts with the vision and goals.

Jeff Bezos, founder of Amazon, exemplifies intentionality by consistently focusing on customer obsession. He crafted a compelling vision of making Amazon "the Earth's most customer-centric company" and communicated this vision effectively throughout the organization. His deliberate strategy of prioritizing customer experience has been a guiding principle in Amazon's growth, influencing every decision and action within the company.

N – Nurture

To nurture means to support, encourage, and foster the growth and development of others. It involves creating a positive environment where team members feel valued, respected, and empowered to reach their full potential. Nurturing leaders invest in their people's personal and professional growth through coaching and mentoring, practicing empathy, and embracing servant leadership—putting the needs of others before their own to help them develop and perform at their best.

- Servant Leadership: Leading by prioritizing the needs of the team, facilitating their development, and removing obstacles to their success.

- Coaching and Mentoring: Providing guidance, knowledge, and support to help team members grow professionally and personally.

- Empathy and Emotional Support: Understanding and sharing the feelings of others to build strong relationships.

Satya Nadella, CEO of Microsoft, nurtured a culture of empathy and learning by embracing servant leadership. He invested in his employees' development through coaching and mentoring programs, promoting a growth mindset, and encouraging collaboration. This approach revitalized the company's innovative spirit and employee engagement.

S – Self-Awareness

Self-awareness is the conscious knowledge of one's own character, feelings, motives, desires, strengths, and weaknesses. It's about understanding how one's behavior affects others and being mindful of one's impact as a leader. Self-aware leaders embrace vulnerability and authenticity, openly acknowledging their limitations and mistakes. Use tools like AcuMax, DISC, or Strength Finder assessment tools to build a better understanding of yourself. This openness fosters trust and creates a culture where others feel safe to do the same.

- Vulnerability: Willingness to be open about challenges and uncertainties, which fosters deeper connections.

- Authenticity: Being true to oneself and consistent in actions and words, building credibility and trust.

- Emotional Intelligence: Recognizing and managing one's own emotions and understanding those of others.

Brené Brown, a researcher and storyteller, emphasizes the power of vulnerability in leadership. She argues that vulnerability is not a weakness but a strength that inspires trust and connection. By sharing her own vulnerabilities and encouraging others to do the same, she has inspired leaders worldwide to embrace authenticity, leading to stronger connections and more resilient organizations.

P – Purpose

Purpose is the underlying reason behind your

actions—the compelling "why" that drives you and your organization. A clear and meaningful purpose inspires and motivates others by connecting their work to a larger mission or cause. Purpose-driven leaders practice servant leadership, aligning their actions with core values and focusing on the greater good rather than personal gain.

- Mission Alignment: Ensuring that individual and team objectives support the overarching mission of the organization.

- Values-Based Leadership: Leading in a way that reflects core values and principles, fostering a sense of meaning and fulfillment.

- Community Impact: Emphasizing the broader impact of the organization's work on society and stakeholders.

Paul Polman, former CEO of Unilever, embedded sustainability and social responsibility into the company's core purpose. By focusing on making a positive impact on the world, he inspired employees and stakeholders to work toward shared, meaningful goals.

Influence In Action™

I – Influence

Influence is the capacity to have an effect on the character, development, or behavior of someone or something. Inspirational leaders positively shape the thoughts and actions of others through their behavior, communication, and example. Effective influence relies on strong communication skills, the ability to build trust through authenticity, and demonstrating vulnerability to connect on a deeper level.

- Effective Communication: Conveying messages clearly, persuasively, and in a way that resonates emotionally.

- Relationship Building: Establishing strong connections based on trust, respect, and mutual understanding.

- Modeling Behavior: Leading by example, embodying the qualities and work ethic you expect from others.

Nelson Mandela once said, "It is better to lead from behind and to put others in front, especially when you celebrate victory when nice things occur. You take the front line when there is danger. Then people will appreciate your leadership." This principle of leadership by example is key to inspiring others. People are more likely to follow a leader who embodies the values and actions they preach.

R – Resilience

Resilience is the ability to recover quickly from difficulties and adapt to adversity. Resilient leaders maintain focus, optimism, and determination in the face of challenges, setbacks, or failures. They model authenticity by acknowledging hardships while demonstrating the strength to persevere. Resilience involves managing stress effectively, maintaining a positive outlook, and inspiring the same perseverance in others.

- Adaptability: Being flexible and open to change when circumstances shift.

- Emotional Stability: Regulating emotions to remain calm and composed under pressure.

- Learning from Failure: Viewing setbacks as opportunities for growth and encouraging a similar mindset in others.

Sheryl Sandberg, COO of Facebook, demonstrated

resilience after a personal tragedy. By openly sharing her experiences and vulnerability, she inspired others to overcome their own challenges and fostered a culture of support and resilience within the organization.

E – Empower

To empower means to give others the authority, confidence, and resources to take initiative and make decisions. Empowered team members are more engaged, innovative, and committed because they feel trusted and valued. Empowering leaders engage in coaching and mentoring, providing guidance while allowing autonomy. They practice servant leadership by focusing on developing others and enabling them to succeed independently.

- Delegation and Trust: Assigning responsibilities and trusting team members to carry them out.

- Coaching and Mentoring: Guiding team members in developing their skills and confidence.

- Encouraging Autonomy: Allowing individuals to make decisions and take ownership of their work.

Susan Wojcicki, CEO of YouTube, empowers her

team by promoting a culture of innovation and autonomy. She encourages employees to take risks and supports them through coaching and mentorship, fostering an environment where creative ideas thrive.

By embracing these principles, leaders can create a transformative impact on their organizations, leading with both the mind and the heart to truly INSPIRE those around them.

The **INSPIRE** acronym embodies leadership qualities that harmoniously engage the three key regions of the brain—the neocortex, limbic brain, and motor brain—to create transformational and sustainable leadership. Each element of INSPIRE interacts with these brain regions to foster effective leadership behaviors and organizational success.

- Neocortex (Conscious Mind): Responsible for strategic thinking, planning, and decision-making. It is engaged through elements like Intentionality, where leaders set clear visions and goals, and Self-Awareness, where leaders reflect on their actions and adjust accordingly.

- Limbic Brain (Emotional Center): Governs emotions, motivation, and social connections. It is activated through Nurture, Purpose, and Resilience, fostering strong emotional bonds, motivating teams, and managing stress and setbacks.

- Motor Brain (Habit Formation Center): Comprises structures like the basal ganglia and cerebellum, responsible for habit formation and automating behaviors. It comes into play through Empowerment, where leaders help team members develop new skills and habits through autonomous action.

The forgotten link in this synergy is the connection between the neocortex and the motor brain. This link represents how conscious, intentional actions and strategic plans formulated in the neocortex are transformed into automatic, habitual behaviors by the motor brain. Through consistent repetition and practice, the deliberate choices and behaviors advocated by the leader become ingrained in the organization's daily operations. This transformation ensures that the leader's vision and strategies are not just temporary initiatives but become a lasting part of the organizational culture and practices.

In essence, **INSPIRE** bridges the gap between intentional leadership and habitual action. By understanding and leveraging the connection between the neocortex and the motor brain—the forgotten link—leaders can effectively translate their strategic intentions into sustained behaviors and habits within their teams, leading to enduring success and impact.

<u>www.empowermindset.coach</u>

About Your Co-Author

Mr. Verma is a sought-after **Leadership Coach**, **Transformation Leader**, and **Entrepreneur** with over 27 years of experience in IT, management consulting, operations, and executive coaching. His career journey with industry giants like IBM, Capgemini, and Tata Motors has shaped his deep expertise in leadership, team optimization, and driving business success.

Known for his results-driven coaching style, Mr. Verma empowers **CEOs, business owners, and high-performing executives** to achieve breakthrough success without burnout. His proven **Smart Success Systems** are grounded in science-backed methodologies and deliver measurable results, helping his clients optimize performance, lead with impact, and unlock their full potential.

During his corporate career, Mr. Verma managed multimillion-dollar projects and global teams across industries, cultivating a fascination with understanding why certain individuals and teams outperform others. This curiosity led him on a transformative quest to explore the key drivers of success. After studying under renowned thought leaders like Dr. John Maxwell, Dr. Daniel Amen, Dr. Joseph McLendon III, and Paul Martinelli, as well as immersing himself in over 100 books on leadership and mindset, Mr. Verma identified **mindset** as the critical differentiator between ordinary and extraordinary success.

As the **Chief Coach and Mentor** at Empower Mindset, Mr. Verma helps leaders build self-awareness, develop actionable strategies, and create sustainable systems for success.

His coaching philosophy centers on three guiding principles:

1. **You cannot improve what you cannot measure.**
2. **Success is a result of systems, not luck.**
3. **What works for one person may not work for another.**

This personalized, systems-oriented approach has enabled Mr. Verma to transform his own life—reversing type 2 diabetes, building a multi-million-dollar business, and co-founding an innovative AI company that automates technical bid evaluations in the Oil and Gas industry.

In addition to coaching, Mr. Verma shares his expertise as the host of the popular podcast **"Empower Your Mind for Success"** and as the creator of **The Science of Inspiration Summit**, where he interviews leading authors, entrepreneurs, and influencers. His mission is to help leaders harness the power of self-awareness and inspiration to drive meaningful, long-lasting change in their organizations and lives.

At IBM and Capgemini, Mr. Verma excelled as a Client Partner, aligning client priorities with strategic transformation initiatives. His expertise in sales, marketing, digital engineering, and global program delivery has earned him a reputation for delivering exceptional value and innovative solutions in complex business environments.

Mr. Verma's coaching delivers tangible results:

- **Clarity and confidence** to lead effectively under pressure.
- **Systematic frameworks** for achieving goals without sacrificing well-being.
- **Enhanced team dynamics** and leadership capabilities to inspire peak performance.

Based in Detroit, MI, Mr. Verma enjoys life with his wife, Pallavi, their daughters, Mahek and Sarahi, and their energetic Wheaten Terrier, Milo. When he's not coaching or speaking, you'll find him on the tennis court or cheering for the Detroit Lions.

Learn more about Mr. Verma's transformative coaching services at Empower Mindset.

www.empowermindset.coach

Chapter Four:
Don't Trust the Process, Trust the Results

In Chapter One, I wrote, "The setting of high expectations is key. Most businesspeople do the opposite. They set out to "manage expectations" merely by setting low expectations. If there was ever a recipe for failure, this is it. The best business comes from setting high expectations and meeting or exceeding those expectations."

"Trust the process" is just another way of saying "Don't expect much in the way of results." On May 14, 2013, former Philadelphia 76ers general manager and president of basketball operations Sam Hinkie said, "We talk a lot about the process, not the outcome. And trying to consistently take all the best information you can and consistently make good decisions. Sometimes they work, and sometimes they don't, but you reevaluate them all."

From this anti-competitive stance, "Trust the process" was born. Over the next several years, it became the 76ers rallying cry…or excuse, when looked at objectively.

Robert J. Smith, MFA

Here are the 76ers regular season records under Hinkie's "Trust the process" philosophy:

Season:	Record:
2013-2014	19-63
2014-2015	18-64
2015-2016	10-72

3 Seasons: 47 wins and 199 losses equals a .191 winning percentage. 152 games under .500.

Here are the 76ers regular-season records since they moved away from Hinkie's "Trust the process" philosophy:

Season:	Record:
2016-2017	28-54
2017-2018	52-30
2018-2019	51-31
2019-2020	43-30
2020-2021	49-23
2021-2022	51-31
2022-2023	54-28

Influence In Action™

2023-2024   47-35

8 Seasons: 375 Wins and 262 Losses equals a .589 winning percentage. 113 games <u>over</u> .500.

The first season, away from a process focus to a results focus, showed an immediate improvement with a gain of 18 games in the win column. Every season since the 76ers have owned a winning record.

The results are irrefutable. "Trust the process" is a losing philosophy.

Results are the only viable, real-world measurement. There are no moral victories in business.

Winning matters. Skillsets matter. As I tell my clients, "We should always work to build momentum. Success fuels passion for more success." Don't take it from me. Take it from a man who is arguably the greatest hitter in the history of Major League Baseball.

"Baseball, to me, was more work than play. In fact, it was all work. You see, I was lucky enough to lead the league when I was twenty years old. After that, I wanted to lead it every year." -Ty Cobb

Robert J. Smith, MFA

Did that philosophy work for him? You bet! Ty Cobb led the American League in hitting for 12 of his 24 prolific seasons.

I use the very same philosophy in my system for Entrepreneur Pitch mentoring with everyone from high school, college, and grad school students to current professionals. I expect my mentees to win, and they do. The plan is that once they get a taste for winning, they never lose their thirst for winning.

So far, we are batting a thousand. Our mentees and students of all ages have earned thousands in Entrepreneur Pitch Competitions. Here is our youngest student, Davina Horowitz, as mentioned in our Prologue.

Don't "Trust the process." Trust the results. Your clients, family, and friends will all appreciate it. So will you.

Influence In Action™

Joanne Glenn, Pasco County Teacher of the Year, Chad Mallo, Davina Horowitz, Jaysa Boyer-Tushaus, and Your Author

https://www.johncmaxwellgroup.com/RobertJSmith

Robert J. Smith, MFA

Chapter Five:
Mindset of a Leader:
Foundations for Success

Author: Leelan Rodriguez

The past two years have tested everything I know about leadership. I've faced challenges that demanded more than just knowledge; they required strength, resolve, and a commitment to principles that carried me through my toughest trials. My journey didn't start with my accident, but it certainly amplified what I'd already learned about leadership.

On October 16, 2022, I broke my neck in a motorcycle accident. At the hospital, the doctor told me that without immediate surgery, I would die. Even if I survived, he said, I'd likely be paralyzed below the neck. At that moment, I made a promise—to him and to myself: "One day, I will walk again." Nearly two years later, on October 15, 2024, I took my first steps. Those steps weren't just about recovery—they were a testament to the mindset and principles I've put into action.

I'm not sharing these insights as someone who has maintained a successful business nor as someone with decades in the field. I'm sharing them as someone breaking into the world of entrepreneurship, bringing forward principles I believe can serve anyone willing to apply them. My hope is that these lessons—tested and amplified through adversity—resonate with you, no matter where you are in your journey.

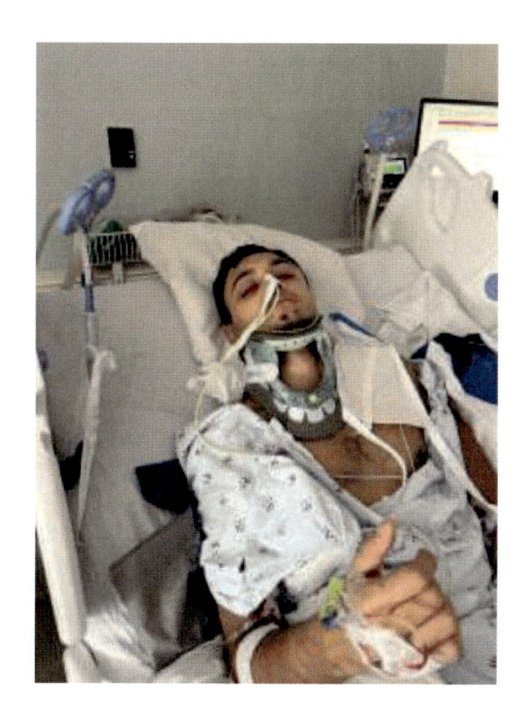

Robert J. Smith, MFA

Creating and maintaining your vision

A vision is a powerful tool for leaders, acting as a guiding star that outlines where an organization is headed and what it aims to achieve. It serves as both a goal and a belief system that shapes decision-making and inspires action. Developing a vision begins with reflecting on personal and organizational values to understand what you want to accomplish and why it matters. Once established, a vision must be communicated clearly and consistently to motivate team members to rally behind a common purpose.

A compelling vision becomes particularly vital during tough times, serving as a source of strength when challenges arise. It helps leaders and their teams navigate uncertainty, reinforcing the idea that acknowledging vulnerabilities can enhance effectiveness. By fostering an environment where struggles are recognized, leaders can create a culture of trust and innovation, transforming challenges into opportunities for growth.

For many months after my accident, my vision revolved around keeping the promise to the doctor that I would one day walk again. However, as time passed and I struggled to see progress, I fell into a deep depression. For every small victory I achieved, it felt as if there were three setbacks waiting to pull me down. During that difficult period, I had a pivotal realization: my deeper goal was to avoid being a burden to myself, my family, and society. This insight led me to create a new vision: to embrace and enjoy life as it is and to help others recognize that their "disabilities"—whether visible or not—can be their greatest strengths. By developing a clear vision, leaders empower themselves and their teams to transform their own challenges into strengths, fostering resilience and creating a shared sense of purpose within the organization.

In conclusion, a strong vision is not just about achieving personal goals; it is about inspiring and uplifting those around us. As we navigate our journeys, remember that our visions can evolve, and through them, we can empower others to transform their challenges into their greatest strengths. The ability to create and maintain a vision is the cornerstone of effective leadership, guiding us through both light and darkness.

Resilience and Perseverance

A clear vision serves as the guiding force that keeps leaders and their teams on course. But even the strongest vision requires resilience and perseverance to withstand challenges. These qualities fuel the journey, allowing leaders to face obstacles with unwavering dedication to their purpose.

Resilience and perseverance sustain essential leadership qualities like gratitude, accountability, and team management. Without resilience, a leader cannot recover from setbacks; without perseverance, they cannot push forward when the road becomes difficult. Together, these traits allow leaders to grow stronger through challenges. Great leaders embrace trials not because they enjoy them but because they recognize the growth opportunities they present.

Not only have I been challenged personally, but in the professional realm as well. About eight months after my accident, I became a youth director for Door of Hope Youth and Family Resource Center, where financial struggles were a constant challenge. Like many nonprofits, we relied heavily on grants and donations to survive, and the difficulties of securing grants often put us in a tough spot. But resilience meant refusing to let these limitations stall our mission, and perseverance meant finding ways to keep moving forward.

To overcome some financial obstacles. With my RBA (return-based assessment) certification, I proposed plans to connect with local businesses, high schools, and colleges, creating partnerships to fulfill our staffing needs through volunteer support. These connections provided crucial resources when funding was limited, reinforcing that resilience is not just about enduring pressure; it's about pushing through with creativity and determination, building community, and staying strong when stability is out of reach.

Leadership is not determined by a title or external achievements—it is about how you handle challenges. My journey has shown me that resilience and perseverance are essential to effective leadership. I would rather endure this path, with all its difficulties, than miss the invaluable lessons that have deepened my understanding of strength and purpose.

Gratitude

Resilience provides the strength to push through challenges, and gratitude brings a valuable perspective, allowing leaders to find appreciation even in difficult moments. Together, these qualities shape a leader's mindset and foster a positive environment for both personal and team growth.

Gratitude is a powerful mindset for effective leadership. It creates a positive environment where people feel valued, even when leaders remain firm, disciplined, and serious. Gratitude is not about leniency; it is about showing appreciation for those who contribute to a leader's growth and success. When team members feel appreciated, they are more loyal and motivated, which is essential in any business environment. But gratitude should also extend inward. Leaders often tend to be their own harshest critics. Learning to appreciate one's personal growth and efforts can be a transformative practice, helping build inner strength and compassion, ultimately creating a well-rounded individual.

I met Eric during my rehabilitation at Rancho Los Amigos. He was only 14 years old and had a passion for building pocket bike engines. One day, he decided to ride one of these small bikes down a hill, reaching speeds of *sixty* miles per hour. As he crossed an intersection, he collided with a truck. The impact broke nearly every bone in his body. Eric fell into a coma and was placed on life support. Doctors advised his mother to pull the plug, saying he would remain in a vegetative state for life. But she refused, believing in his survival.

Miraculously, Eric woke up, defying the odds. I do not know the details of how he woke up or what he felt, but I do know that he faces life with a spirit of gratitude despite his limitations. Confined to a hospital bed and requiring constant care, Eric once told me, "The doctor was going to kill me. But I made it out alive. And I am just so grateful to be alive." Hearing those words from someone so young, who had lost so much, profoundly impacted me. On days when I struggle to get out of bed or push through the pain, I remember Eric's words: "I am alive. I am grateful to be alive."

Eric's story serves as a reminder that gratitude is not about having perfect circumstances; it is about finding appreciation even in adversity. Entrepreneurs and leaders face challenges—setbacks, financial difficulties, and failures—that test their strength. But gratitude transforms these obstacles into opportunities for growth. It builds resilience and allows leaders to focus on the value of each experience and the loyalty of their teams. If a 14-year-old boy facing severe limitations can find something to be grateful for, then as leaders, we can choose to see the value in our journey and the people who walk it with us.

Gratitude is a choice—a practice that leaders can integrate into their lives. Taking time each day to reflect on three things you are grateful for, whether it is the support of a team member, the opportunity to learn from a setback, or your own perseverance, can transform how you approach challenges. Expressing appreciation to those around you and to yourself builds stronger relationships and creates a culture of loyalty and collaboration. Eric's story reminds me that gratitude is not just a feeling; it is a mindset that shapes our character, builds resilience, and strengthens our leadership from the inside out.

Accountability

While gratitude helps leaders value the journey, accountability ensures they take full responsibility for every choice and outcome. Effective leadership is built on the trust that accountability creates, both within the leader and with those they lead.

Accountability is at the core of effective leadership,

applying just as much to life-altering moments as it does to running a business. On the day of my accident, although I was not legally at fault, I failed to follow a crucial, unwritten rule that every motorcyclist should know: Do not ride in the right lane when approaching a four-way intersection. Cars can turn unexpectedly, and by riding in that lane, I placed myself in a vulnerable position. The one person responsible for keeping me safe on the road—the one my family depended on—was me, and I failed.

As a leader, especially in business, it is not just about knowing the rules; it is about having the discipline to apply them consistently, even when it is inconvenient or seemingly harmless to ignore them. Just as I was responsible for my own safety on that motorcycle, business owners are responsible for the safety and success of their companies. The actions they take or fail to take—no matter how small—can have significant consequences.

I accept that lifelong consequences from my accident—my rehabilitation, the impact on my family, the life changes—stemmed from my choice. In business, this is akin to a leader taking full responsibility for a project's failure or a company's downturn, even when external factors play a role. It is not about guilt; it is about ownership and growth.

Business like motorcycling, involves taking risks. Success does not come from avoiding these risks but from facing them responsibly. Leaders who embody accountability build resilience and trust, creating a culture where growth is possible, even through challenges and uncertainties.

Calculated Risk-Taking

Accountability sets a solid foundation, enabling leaders to make decisions with integrity and forethought. This level of responsibility is crucial when taking calculated risks—bold actions guided by careful consideration and a commitment to growth.

Taking calculated risks is about understanding the stakes, weighing the consequences, and choosing to act, even with uncertainty ahead. In my journey, I have learned that taking risks is not about being reckless; it is about trusting your instincts and committing to action, even when others may not fully understand your choices.

During my rehabilitation at Rancho Los Amigos, I

was often labeled as "impulsive." I would transfer myself from my bed to my chair or, on one occasion, leave my unit without required supervision, nearly prompting the sheriffs to be called to locate me. These actions led to increased monitoring, including a 24/7 camera in my room. But I didn't see my actions as impulsive; to me, they were necessary. I knew the potential risks—another injury that could leave me bedridden again, prolonging my healing. For the hospital, the stakes were significant as well: extensive paperwork, reputational loss, lawsuits, or, most concerning to me, disciplinary actions against staff members responsible for my supervision if I got hurt. Still, I needed to push beyond limitations and test my independence if I was ever going to regain a normal life.

Just eight months after my accident—a time when I was just beginning to adjust to my body—I took on the role of Youth Director for Door of Hope Youth and Family Resource Center, determined to make a meaningful impact in my community. The role brought immense pressure, requiring me to look and act in a certain way to meet the expectations I set for myself. I was averaging only eight to ten hours of sleep a week, pushing myself every day to prove that my disability does not define my limits. Eventually, as the lack of sleep and physical strain began affecting my ability to give my best, I made the difficult decision to step down—not as a failure, but as a necessary adjustment to protect my health and future.

For leaders and entrepreneurs, success often means taking risks without guaranteed outcomes. It is about daring to act, trusting yourself to manage the challenges, and making necessary adjustments along the way. Equally important is accepting accountability for those choices—recognizing when to push forward and when to step back. In my case, stepping down was an act of accountability, a decision to prioritize both my health and my commitment to those I served.

Team Management

"The eye cannot say to the hand, 'I don't need you!' And the head cannot say to the feet, 'I don't need you!' On the contrary, those parts of the body that seem to be weaker are indispensable, and the parts that we think are less honorable we treat with special honor. And the parts that are unpresentable are treated with special modesty, while our presentable parts need no special

treatment. But God has put the body together, giving greater honor to the parts that lacked it, so that there should be no division in the body, but that its parts should have equal concern for each other. If one part suffers, every part suffers with it; if one part is honored, every part rejoices with it."

— 1 Corinthians 21-26

Calculated risks drive progress, but effective team management ensures those risks are managed wisely and collaboratively. A well-led team amplifies a leader's vision, creating strength in unity and transforming potential obstacles into shared achievements. I am not here to push a biblical agenda, but this passage aligns perfectly with the essence of team management. No role is too small, and no role too big. Everyone depends on each other to get the job done, and every contribution is essential for success. Team management is the cornerstone of any successful organization. A well-led team can achieve more than the sum of its parts, and cultivating this dynamic is crucial for any leader. My leadership experience as a youth director and at Southeast Academy Military and Law Enforcement High School gave me a solid foundation in effective team management.

At Southeast Academy, I served as both a Squad Leader and Alpha Company GSD. As a Squad Leader, I managed ten cadets, focusing on drill proficiency, uniform standards, and time management. I also provided academic accountability, ensuring cadets met their standards. This role required me to develop communication skills, motivate my team, and balance responsibilities. I learned the importance of planning, feedback, and creating a positive team culture—fundamental elements of effective management.

Influence In Action™

In my role as Alpha Company GSD, I oversaw operations at the company level, managing logistical tasks like ceremonies, equipment, and event setups. My team included five other leaders: the Company Commander (CC), Company Executive Officer (CXO), Company First Sergeant (CFS), Company Adjutant (CA), and Company Guide (CG). Each of us had distinct responsibilities, and close coordination was essential to our shared goals.

When setting up events, the scope varied—some were exclusive to our company of one hundred fifty cadets, while others required coordination across the school of over three hundred cadets, meaning that there had to be collaboration between Alpha and Bravo Company GSD and the Battalion GSD, who oversaw higher-level operations. This experience taught me teamwork, adaptability, project management, and proactive problem-solving.

As the Youth Director for Door of Hope Youth and Family Resource Center, I oversaw leadership facilitation for students, families, and mentors. Part of my role involved assigning a mentor to each student. Each mentor was administered a DISC behavioral personality test so that we could better understand their strengths and weaknesses, which helped me match students with the most suitable mentors. My role was to ensure that students were set up for success, equipping them with skills to become leaders in their communities and homes. This experience reinforced the importance of understanding each person's strengths and aligning them with a common goal. Whether managing a diverse group cadet or leading a group of mentors, the lesson remains the same—effective leadership requires recognizing the strengths of every member and guiding them toward a shared mission.

Holistic Approach to Leadership

Successful team management goes beyond roles, recognizing each individual's unique value. This holistic approach to leadership fosters respect and understanding, where team members are supported as whole individuals.

Holistic leadership is about creating an environment where people feel valued beyond their roles and supported in both their personal and professional growth. When you lead with genuine care, you build a foundation where trust grows and collaboration thrives.

One leader who embodies this idea is Dave Ramsey.

He shared a story about keeping a team member on the payroll for two years while she battled cancer, even though she was unable to work. For him, the bottom line was not just the business but the people behind it. Because he could afford to, he took care of her financially. However, holistic leadership requires a fine balance—if you focus only on the business, you risk losing team morale, while being too emotionally invested can impact the organization's stability. Effective holistic leadership lies in balancing the needs of people with those of the business.

    I understand what makes an organization thrive. At Southeast Academy, I focused on building relationships grounded in respect and care. As a big brother figure, they often sought my approval, but my main goal was to guide them toward accomplishing things for themselves. I wanted them to see that while my support was there, the true reward was in their own sense of fulfillment, growth, and belief in their leadership. This approach led to my receiving Southeast Academy's highest honor, the Leadership Award, chosen by both the senior class and faculty. Only one student each year receives this award for best representing the school's definition of leadership, and I am proud to share that honor with my friend Bryan Sarto.

Just this past year, as I returned to Southeast Academy to mentor students, I met Bryan as he began his senior year. I had the privilege of walking alongside him, building a relationship, counseling him, witnessing his growth, and, most importantly, becoming friends. Now, he's a cadet at the New Mexico Military Institute (NMMI) in Roswell, New Mexico—a prestigious military junior college and high school known for its rigorous academic and leadership training. NMMI's demanding standards foster academic excellence, leadership, and physical fitness, preparing students for further education and leadership roles. The fact that Bryan has earned his place there is a testament to his character and commitment, and I am honored to continue walking with him on his journey into adulthood. My hope is that, in guiding others to see their own potential, I can inspire a ripple effect of purposeful, people-centered leadership.

At Breakneck Leadership & Team Management Consulting, we are dedicated to fostering genuine leadership and inspiring real change.

I have pursued several key certifications that equip

me to have influence:

John Maxwell's Leader, Speaker, and Coaching Certification: This program has enhanced my ability to mentor others, focusing on practical personal growth in leadership.

Return-Based Accountability (RBA) Certification: A managing/budgeting framework that I implement to help organizations increase internal capacity, improve performance, and create measurable results for customers and communities.

DISC Behavioral Analysis Trainer: This certification equips me to understand and apply the DISC model of human behavior, enabling me to assess personality styles, enhance communication, and improve teamwork within organizations."

Even though I am no longer the Youth Director for Door of Hope Youth and Family Resource Center, I continue to collaborate with them to support families and engage the community. I plan to increase my involvement in the upcoming school year with some exciting initiatives.

At Breakneck Leadership, we believe every

interaction matters. We foster hope, accountability, and empowerment, enabling individuals to grow into valuable assets in their communities and effective leaders in their homes. We aim to create a ripple effect—when one person thrives, everyone around them benefits.

Reflecting on these past two years, I realize that if given the choice, I would rather break my neck every day than lose the powerful insights this journey has intensified. The experience forged and deepened lessons I had already learned, shaping my understanding of leadership in ways I never imagined. Principles like vision, resilience, gratitude, and accountability aren't just ideals; they're practical tools that drive meaningful growth and build solid foundations. I may be new to the field of entrepreneurship, but these insights, tested through adversity, can resonate with anyone dedicated to creating a legacy. Whether you're an established business owner or just beginning your path, I hope the perspectives I've shared inspire you to see your own challenges as sources of strength and to lead with purpose. Together, we can cultivate not just successful businesses but resilient, people-centered legacies that endure."

Influence In Action™

Scan the QR code to connect with Breakneck Leadership & Team Management Consulting and explore how these principles can support your journey. If you're in the Los Angeles area, let's take this conversation further— I'd love to connect and discuss how we can make an impact together.

https://www.linkedin.com/in/leelan-rodriguez-103bab243/

Robert J. Smith, MFA

About Your Co-Author

Leelan Rodriguez is the dynamic founder of Breakneck Leadership & Team Management Consulting. He's on a mission to help individuals and teams build resilience while embracing purpose-driven leadership. With a knack for turning challenges into stepping stones, Leelan provides actionable strategies that foster genuine growth and development.

Leelan's leadership adventure kicked off at the Southeast Academy of Military and Law Enforcement High

School, where he sharpened essential skills in team management, problem-solving, and mentorship. His enthusiasm for nurturing talent didn't stop there; he took on the role of Youth Director at the Door of Hope Youth and Family Resource Center, where he collaborated with dedicated teams to roll out impactful programs for young people and families.

But Leelan's expertise doesn't just come from experience—it's backed by a list web 2 of professional certifications. He is a Maxwell Leadership Certified Team Member, Speaker, and Coach (MLCT), a skilled DISC Trainer, and holds certification in Return-Based Assessment (RBA). These accolades not only establish his credibility but also arm him with the essential tools to help others master impactful leadership skills that result in tangible success.

At the heart of Leelan's mission is his belief in the transformative power of personal experiences. By helping individuals recognize their unique journeys, he empowers them to make a positive difference in their communities.

In essence, Leelan Rodriguez is more than just a consultant; he's a true catalyst for change. He's dedicated to cultivating a new generation of resilient leaders ready to tackle any obstacle that comes their way. If you're eager to boost your own leadership skills—or those of your team—his practical and strategic approach is your roadmap to success. Don't miss this chance to turn challenges into opportunities for greatness!

Chapter Six:
The One Thing™

A very popular writing and speaking topic is 'facing and overcoming adversity.' Those stories are easily available. Some are inspiring. Some are not. There are also plenty of other stories here and elsewhere that may be able to motivate you to ACTION. There are plenty of people with inspiring stories. Leelan and Steven's stories for example, show just what unwavering commitment to persevere regardless of circumstance can do for a person.

Here is my condensed story of facing and overcoming adversity:

After a couple of not-at-fault motor vehicle accidents that resulted in debilitating spinal injuries, I was briefly unable to walk. And then, for a longer period of time, I was unable to walk without the assistance of two canes. I was told by 25 neurosurgeons that I may never "walk normally" again. Nevertheless, I persevered through 14 surgeries and decades of physical therapy, and I'm happy to say that I am back to walking without assistance. So what? Maybe the full story would help some of you overcome adversity. If my story will help you, please feel free to contact me and I will be happy to share it with you.

Instead of reading about me, let's think about you and what you are able to accomplish! I believe that will be more helpful to your business and your family. What could make the biggest difference for you? In my forty years of consulting experience, I find that there is usually One Thing™ that makes all the difference in the world. In most cases, all it takes is One Thing™ that get it done for people just like you, me, and everyone else.

The trouble is that One Thing™ is sometimes difficult to identify. It's nearly impossible to identify on our own. It takes a proven process to identify exactly what that One Thing™ is. This is what we offer to all of our consulting clients. An outside view and a proven process to help clients find that One Thing™ they've been searching for. In essence, The One Thing™ that is the difference-maker.

In my decades of experience, I've found that any One of a handful of Things can make all the difference for the majority of the people I have met. The trouble is in taking the time to properly diagnose both the problems and the opportunities that each person faces. Making the correct diagnosis comes from the experience of interviewing and assessing thousands of people, just like you.

We all know that one pill does not cure every ill. In one case, it's simply a matter of gaining credibility by having their story told on major television networks that can propel their business. E.g., Our financial advisory agencies were able to increase advisor income by an average of $85,000.00 with this One Thing™ alone.

In other cases, writing a chapter in a #1 Best Seller has been One Thing™ to make all of the difference to turn struggling businesses into thriving enterprises.

In my case, *THE ADVENTURES OF INSURANCEMAN©were* the One Thing™ that transformed my top-tier financial practice to #1 worldwide rankings. This is why we've created the opportunity for people in every industry to take full advantage of One Thing™ that makes all the difference. The One Thing™a take anyone from good to great!

No competent physician would ever claim that one

pill can cure every ill. And no competent physician would ever prescribe anything without a proper evaluation and work up. Doing so would be tantamount to malpractice.

While The One Thing™ can make all the difference in the world for most people, that One Thing™ is usually different for different people. My mission is to find that One Thing™ for each and every individual.

That One Thing™ that will make all the difference in the world for you and your family.

Schedule your 20-minute free consultation through the link or QR code below to properly diagnose your situation and find The One Thing™ that can immediately increase your sales, revenues, and profits!

https://SmithProfits.com

Chapter Seven:
Mentoring Matters

I've been volunteering my time in elementary schools, middle schools, high schools, colleges, and universities since Ashley, Austin, and Sabrina were in elementary school. I continue to volunteer to this day as Sharon continues to teach.

I have fond memories of working as an adjunct faculty teaching the Certified Financial Planner curriculum to financial professionals at Oglethorpe University. I have even fonder memories of Sabrina assisting me in volunteering to teach both students and parents at Clark Atlanta University.

This time last year, I was at Angeline Academy of Innovation by invitation of Pasco County Teacher of the Year, Chad Mallo. He was referred to me by J.J. Kubski, a parent of one of his students. While I've never met Ms. Kubski, she's familiar with my work through our social media connection and thought enough of it to recommend me.

Robert J. Smith, MFA

After speaking on the importance of presenting with authority, I was asked to judge the school's Entrepreneurial Pitch Competition. I recommended Kevin Harrington, whom Sharon and I have known for more than ten years, as another judge. When it came time for the competition, I was introduced to yet another judge, Frank Nunez, a Program Planner/Kennedy Fellow At The University of South Florida.

After seeing all of the well-prepared students make outstanding pitches, it was unanimous between the three of us and the other judges that one presentation stood out. That presentation was made by 14-year-old student Davina Horowitz, who earned First Place.

Of course, we all provided immediate input as to what we thought she did very well and where improvements could be made for her regional competition and beyond. As our student is a minor, all additional mentoring was accomplished through her teacher, Chad Mallo. In essence, we all served as informal Advisory Board members.

Knowing the importance of displaying authority, as we initially discussed months prior in my initial presentation at AAI, Davina included photos of Kevin and me, along with

Influence In Action™

a USF doctor in scrubs and her engineering teacher in her presentation. As we watched her present in her regional competition, she displayed her Advisory Boardslide. She had to stop her presentation while she received a standing ovation.

MEET OUR ADVISORY BOARD

Kevin Harrington — Original Shark from Shark Tank Marketing Advisory

Dr. Erik Rauch — Platinum Award Winning Medical/USF Nurse Anesthesiology Program

Dr. Robert J. Smith — Writer/Forbes magazine Financial Advisor

Loc Hoang — Engineering professional Engineering/Construction of Product Advisory

It was at that very moment that we knew she had one with the competition. It was her hard work and dedication, along with her novel idea, that drove her to win. At the same time, her slide was the difference-maker right at the time when she needed it most. It was The One Thing™ that made all the difference. Of course, The One Thing™ is different for everyone, and it is also may also be different in different situations.

This was just the beginning of a whirlwind 24 hours for Sharon and me. After spending the evening at AAI in support of Davina, we headed to the USF campus in Tampa to stay the night and support our medical and grad school mentees in their statewide Entrepreneur Pitch Competition sponsored by Florida Blue Cross and Blue Shield.

A few weeks earlier, Frank Nunez asked me to mentor several students from across the state for that competition. I quickly developed a four-point process for doing so:

1. First meeting; see and hear their pitch.
2. Offer suggestions and schedule a follow-up meeting.
3. Second meeting: see and hear their pitch again.
4. Offer final suggestions for polishing that pitch.

One mentee, Rachel Chapman, a University of Central Florida medical school student with an undergraduate degree from Harvard, was able to follow that advice to the letter and make all of the necessary refinements. The result? She earned a $10,000.00 award from Florida Blue Cross and Blue Shield to further develop and market her medical device.

The best part is that I was able to introduce Rachel to Davina. Hopefully, they will be friends for life and potentially work together someday!

Davina Horowitz, Rachel Chapman, and Your Author

It's never enough to have a great idea, innovation, product, or service; we must be able to skillfully convey the benefits of using our great ideas, innovations, products, and services.

One of the best ways to do that is as Ringo Starr sings, "With a Little Help from My Friends." Whether or not

Robert J. Smith, MFA

you have been fortunate enough to have a mentor, there is no doubt that being a mentor is one of the most rewarding things you can do.

Chapter Eight:
You Can Judge a Book by Its Cover

Contrary to popular belief, you can indeed judge a book by its cover. In fact, writing a book is a time-tested method for elevating your authority and creating PR opportunities for yourself. The formula for this marketing method is simple. It's as easy as one, two, three:

1. Create visibility and enhance credibility.
2. Gain local and nationwide television coverage.
3. Gain more speaking opportunities, customers and clients.

Here is something that I learned the very first time that I appeared on nationwide television. After my segment, a producer walked me into her office to make a point that she made loud and clear. She opened a closet and scores of books fell out onto the floor, just like sporting goods and other household items fell out of Fibber McGee and Molly's closet on their classic radio and television programs.

The producer said, "These are from all of the authors

trying to get onto our show." Then, she pointed to other books displayed all around her office and asked, "What do these books have in common?" It was obvious from the covers of each of those books that they were all #1 Best Sellers.

The moral of the story is that writing a book will help you create visibility and help you enhance your credibility. Writing a #1 Best Seller will help you gain local and nationwide television coverage. Both should help you gain more speaking opportunities, customers and clients. However, you'll always do better with a #1 Best Seller.

Here is an example from a very recent personal experience:

Only three months ago, I attended a very well-known leadership conference with roughly 2,000 – 3,000 attendees. There were scores of speakers who made presentations over the course of three days. There was something inescapable about the crowd's behavior immediately after the introduction for most of those speakers. As speakers were introduced, people continued talking, stirring their coffee, eating food, and/or looking at their phones and computers. The exception was for speakers who were introduced as "a

Influence In Action™

Best Selling Author." In each and every one of those cases, people stopped talking, eating, drinking, and failing to pay attention. Each and every time a speaker was introduced in this manner, conference attendees paid attention. People sat straight and tall, many at the edge of their seats and many with pen or pencil and notepad in hand. The difference is that they gave the speaker their full and undivided attention. This happened every single time that a speaker was introduced as "a Best Selling Author." Pay attention to the speaker introductions at the next event you attend and see if your experience is the same.

Could this be The One Thing™ that you do that make all the difference in the world in your career and business? If so, we can help you make it happen. We've helped dozens of people reach Best Seller status for the first time, including a retired President of UPS International.

This is also a proven way for speakers to gain more bookings as well as higher-paid bookings. It's also helped speakers gain more clients and sell far more products and services than they did before creating their Best Seller.

Even if you are not a public speaker, you are able to bring in more prospective clients with a Best Seller. After buying or being given a copy of your Best Seller, prospective clients are pre-disposed to do business with you.

Here is a sample #1 Best Seller, the first book in this series, ***INFLUENCE IN ACTION™ GAINS PROVEN RESULTS AND DRIVES SALES***.

VIDEO BOOK TRAILER

It's humbling to see your work rank ahead of your contemporaries. It's beyond humbling to see your work outrank the masters.

INFLUENCE IN ACTION™ GAINS PROVEN RESULTS AND DRIVES SALES.

Smith's ***INFLUENCE IN ACTION™*** series and other Best Selling titles and comic books may be found here:

https://www.amazon.com/author/robertjsmith

Robert J. Smith, MFA

The Foreword for ***INFLUENCE IN ACTION™ GAINS PROVEN RESULTS AND DRIVES SALES*** was written by "The $2 Billion Host," Forbes Riley.

INFLUENCE IN ACTION™ GAINS PROVEN RESULTS AND DRIVES SALES provides you with everything you need to reach #1 in your industry.

This revolutionary book not only tells you how to accomplish more with your work and in your business, but it also provides you the means to accomplish everything you ever wanted to accomplish!

Influence In Action™

All that you have to do is to leverage your **INFLUENCE** by putting your **INFLUENCE IN ACTION™!**

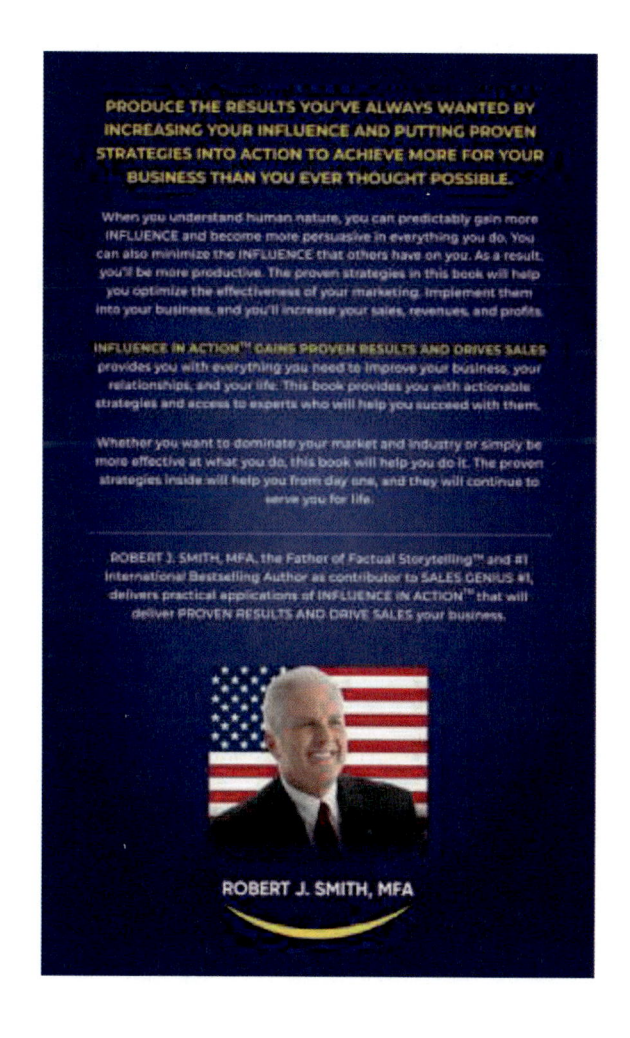

Epilogue

Not only do we have the ability to take ACTION without limitation regardless of our age, health, or other circumstances, we have an obligation to do so. We owe it to our family, friends, and everyone to take consistent ACTION and work to the very best of our abilities.

If there is anything that you've seen from Anish that will help you in your business and in your life, be sure to contact him.

If there is anything that you've seen from Leelan that will help you in your business and in your life, be sure to contact him as well.

As always, feel free to contact me if there is anything I can do to help you.

Whether you are young, old, or in between, we're happy to help you in any way that we can.

No matter your circumstances, we will work to help you improve them.

Our individual and combined aim is to help you make progress. When we can help you make progress, you are better prepared to help your customers and clients make progress. When we can help you make progress, we have done our jobs and done them well.

The choice to take *ACTION* and to put **INFLUENCE IN ACTION™** is up to you.

Robert J. Smith, MFA

"You cannot hope to make progress in areas where you have taken no action."

-**Epictetus**

About Your Author

Robert J. Smith, MFA

Born in metro Detroit, Smith learned to compete at a young age, winning baseball championships in his first season at the age of nine and in his final season at the age of thirty, including a streak of six out of his first eight seasons, all on eight different teams.

His work ethic was developed in his blue-collar beginnings. No one in the history of the Automobile Capital of the World, or in the Great State of Michigan, has completed more oil changes in one day, one week, or one month than Smith has. In fact, he averaged two cars at once from 6:30 a.m. to midnight, seven days per week, for thirty-one straight days during a Mobil Oil recall in the early 1980s. http://www.RobertJSmith.com

After moving to Florida, Smith and another route driver teamed up to complete all of their deliveries after every other route truck driver for Coca-Cola was called back into the warehouse during Hurricane Elena. After developing the #1 home market merchandising route in the Sarasota territory, Smith suffered an on-the-job injury, which led to a career change into the financial services industry.

As a financial services advisor, Smith reached #1 worldwide rankings at AXA Financial, The Equitable, Mutual of New York (MONY), and BankAtlantic/BB&T/SunTrust/Truist. He set records at John Hancock and New York Life. His name is enshrined in a plaque on Madison Avenue. https://SmithProfits.com/

Debilitating spine and other severe injuries necessitated a career change. While undergoing multiple surgeries to regain the ability to walk, he concurrently earned his Master of Fine Arts (MFA) in Creative Writing as Valedictorian at Full Sail University and his Feature Film Writing degree "With Distinction" at UCLA. He holds Director's Awards for "The Art of Visual Storytelling" as well as "Editing for Film, Games and Animation."

Smith's consulting practice helps financial advisors reach the TOP 1% in production, entertainers reach the TOP 1% of Internet Movie Database (IMDb), and every client reaches the top of Google Search Rankings. http://www.RobertJSmithProductions.com

He is an International Best-Selling Author with **SALES GENIUS #1©,** which bested The Wolf of Wall Street's book on sales. **THE ADVENTURES OF INSURANCEMAN©** increase sales for clients and their companies. Smith created **SHORT ATTENTION SPAN DAN©** to teach writing and public speaking to students. Robert J. Smith's Amazon Author Page   After earning his Leadership Certification in Influencing People at the University of Michigan, Smith has turned dozens of businesspeople into #1 International Bestselling Authors.

Smith and his companies have been featured on

Robert J. Smith, MFA

ABC, CBS, CW, FOX, The Golf Channel, NBC, WGN, and hundreds of other media outlets. http://www.IMDb.Me/RobertJSmith

He's been named to the Entrepreneur Magazine Leadership Network and, as a member of the Forbes Business Council, contributed monthly articles to the magazine.

https://www.forbes.com/councils/forbesbusinesscouncil/people/smittyrobertjsmith/

Smith's other book titles in the works include *#1: HOW TO REACH THE VERY TOP IN YOUR INDUSTRY – NO MATTER YOUR PROFESSION, EVERYTHING YOU ALWAYS WANTED TO ABOUT INCREASING BUSINESS* *AND WERE AFRAID TO ASK, INFLUENCE IN ACTION™ BRINGS MORE BUSINESS TO ENTREPRENEURS*, and many others. https://SmithProfits.com/Books/

Smith raised millions for charity and volunteers in public and private schools. Within 24 hours in 2024, one of his high school students and one of his medical school students each won their Entrepreneur Pitch Championships and earned sizable cash prizes to develop each of their medical products that will greatly benefit mankind. He's served as a Field Councilman for the Greater Detroit Area Life Underwriters, Board Member of the Tampa Bay United Way, Treasurer of World League Baseball, and President of the Executive Sports Council. **Robert J. Smith Productions on IMDb**

He lives in Winter Garden, Florida, with Sharon Roznowski and has three children: Ashley, Austin, and Sabrina.

Robert J. Smith, MFA

Coming Soon

INFLUENCE IN ACTION™
TO EDUCATE STUDENTS©

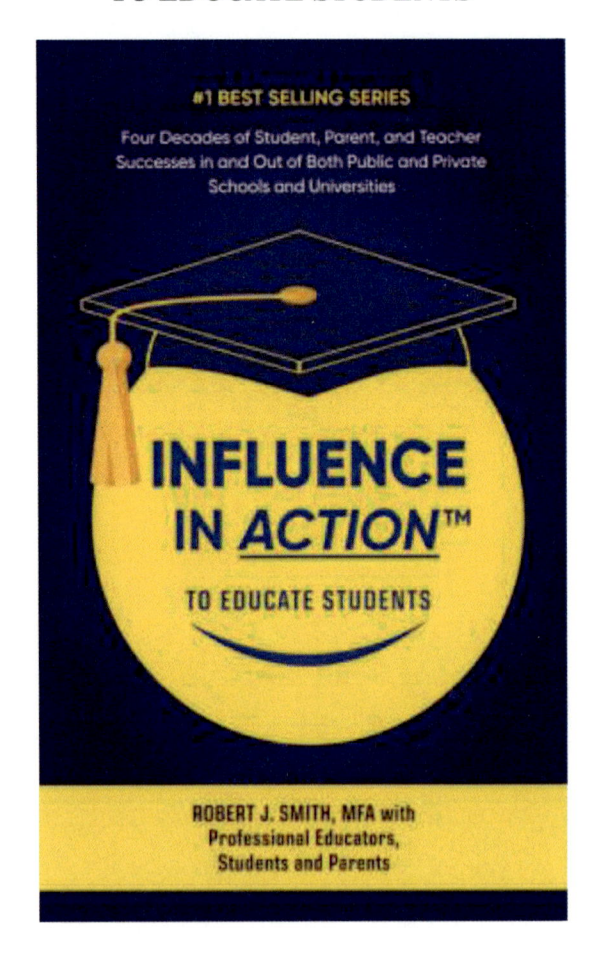

INFLUENCE IN ACTION™
FOR AUTOMOTIVE PROFESSIONALS©

Robert J. Smith, MFA

***INFLUENCE IN ACTION*™**
***FOR SALES PROFESSIONALS*©**

(Cover Coming Soon)

#1:

HOW TO REACH THE TOP IN YOUR INDUSTRY, NO MATTER YOUR PROFESSION©

(Cover Coming Soon)

and

Influence In Action™

EVERYTHING YOU ALWAYS WANTED TO KNOW ABOUT INCREASING BUSINESS*

*AND WERE AFRAID TO ASK

***EXPLAINED BY ROBERT J. SMITH, MFA, AND HIS FORBES ARTICLES*©**

Robert J. Smith, MFA

Coming Soon from *SMITH COMICS:*

THE ADVENTURES OF INSURANCEWOMAN©

REAL ESTATE WOMAN©

REAL ESTATE MAN©

THE AMAZING WEBSITE-MAN©

THE LOAN ARRANGER©

SUPER DENTIST©

SHERRY MASON©

HARRY MASON©

THE ADVENTURES OF BERNIE BURNS©

SHORT ATTENTION SPAN DAN:
THE GREAT HOUDAN©

SHORT ATTENTION SPAN DAN:
WILD THING, YOU MOVE ME©

Influence In Action™

https://SmithProfits.com/

Robert J. Smith, MFA

"Knowledge is of no value unless you put it into action."

-Anton Chekov

Influence In Action™

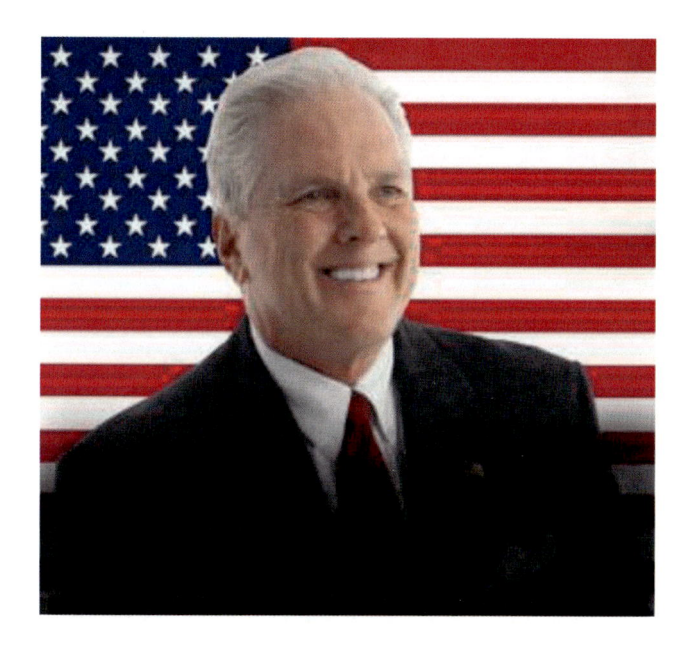

Made in the USA
Middletown, DE
09 January 2025